Pillars of Supervisor Self-Esteem

ANGELA L. ANFIELD &
DAVID J. SAMSON

Copyright © 2013 Pillars of Training, Inc.

All rights reserved.

ISBN: 1495264963
ISBN-13: 978-1495264962

DEDICATION

This book is dedicated to all the people who struggle with the demon of doubt, you are more powerful than you realize.

CONTENTS

CHAPTER 1: INTRODUCTION 1

   Build Self-Confidence & Esteem 2

      What is Self-Confidence? 2

      Building Self-Confidence 3

CHAPTER 2: THOUGHT AWARENESS 7

   What is Thought Awareness? 8

   Rational Thinking 9

   Opportunity Seeking 10

CHAPTER 3: AFFIRMATIONS 12

   Purpose 12

   Giving Praise 13

   Usage 14

   Identification 17

CHAPTER 5: FEAR OF FAILURE 18

   Causes 18

   Symptoms 19

   Overcoming 20

CHAPTER 6: THE PERMA MODEL 22

   About 22

- Usage 23
- Practice 26
- Signs of Impatience 26
- Triggers 27
- Management 27

CHAPTER 8: THE ABC TECHNIQUE 29
- About 29
- Resetting the Pattern 30
- Managing Negative ABC Patterns 30

CHAPTER 9: BURNOUT 33
- What is Burnout? 33
- Symptoms 34
- Stress & Burnout 34
- Avoiding Burnout 35
- Workplace Stress Management 39
  - Reduce Office Noise 39
  - Create a Healthy Workstation 40
  - Clean and Organize Your Office 41
  - Look at Your Commute 41

CHAPTER 1: INTRODUCTION

Self-confidence is extremely important in almost every aspect of our lives, yet so many people struggle to find it. Sadly, this can be a vicious circle: people who lack self-confidence can find it difficult to become successful.

After all, most people are reluctant to back a project that's being pitched by someone who is nervous, fumbling, and overly apologetic. On the other hand, you might be persuaded by someone who speaks clearly, who holds his or her head high, who answers questions assuredly, and who readily admits when he or she does not know something.

Self-confident people inspire confidence in others: their audience, their peers, their bosses, their customers, and their friends. And gaining the confidence of others is one of the key ways in which a self-confident person finds success.

The good news is that self-confidence can be learned and built on. And, whether you're working on your own self-confidence or building the confidence of people around you, it's well worth the effort!

Build Self-Confidence & Esteem

Your level of self-confidence can show in many ways: your behavior, your body language, how you speak, what you say, and so on. Look at the following comparisons of common confident behavior with behavior associated with low self-confidence. Which thoughts or actions do you recognize in yourself and people around you?

Self-Confident	Low Self-Confidence
Doing what you believe to be right, even if others mock or criticize you for it.	Governing your behavior based on what other people think.
Being willing to take risks and go the extra mile to achieve better things.	Staying in your comfort zone, fearing failure, and so avoid taking risks.
Admitting your mistakes, and learning from them.	Working hard to cover up mistakes, and hoping that you can fix the problem before anyone notices.
Extolling your own virtues as often as possible to as many people as possible.	Waiting for others to congratulate you on your accomplishments.
Accepting compliments graciously. "Thanks, I really worked hard on that prospectus. I'm pleased you recognize my efforts."	Dismissing compliments offhandedly. "Oh, that prospectus was nothing really, anyone could have done it."

As you can see from these examples, low self-confidence can be self-destructive, and it often manifests itself as negativity. Self-confident people are generally more positive – they believe in themselves and their abilities, and they also believe in living life to the fullest.

What is Self-Confidence?

Two main things contribute to self-confidence: self-efficacy and self-esteem.

We gain a sense of self-efficacy when we see ourselves (and others similar to ourselves) mastering skills and achieving goals that matter in those skill areas. This is the confidence that, if we learn and work hard in a particular area, we'll succeed. It's this type of confidence that leads people to accept difficult challenges, and persist in the face of setbacks.

This overlaps with the idea of self-esteem, which is a more general sense that we can cope with what's going on in our lives, and that we have a right to be happy. Partly, this comes from a feeling that the people around us approve of us, which we may or may not be able to control. However, it also comes from the sense that we are behaving virtuously, that we're competent at what we do, and that we can compete successfully when we put our minds to it.

Some people believe that self-confidence can be built with affirmations and positive thinking. At Mind Tools, we believe that there's some truth in this, but that it's just as important to build self-confidence by setting and achieving goals – thereby building competence. Without this underlying competence, you don't have self-confidence: you have shallow over-confidence, with all of the upset and failure that this brings.

Building Self-Confidence

So how do you build this sense of balanced self-confidence, founded on a firm appreciation of reality? The bad news is that there's no five-minute solution.

The good news is that building self-confidence is readily achievable, just as long as you have the focus and determination to carry things through. And what's even better is that the things you'll do to build self-confidence will also build success – after all, your confidence will come from real, solid achievement. No-one can take this away from you.

Here are 3 steps to building self-confidence, for which we'll use the metaphor of a journey: preparing for your journey; setting out; and accelerating towards success.

STEP 1: PREPARING FOR YOUR JOURNEY

The first step involves getting yourself ready for your journey to self-confidence. You need to take stock of where you are, think about where you want to go, get yourself in the right mindset for your journey, and commit yourself to starting it and staying with it.

PILLARS OF SUPERVISOR SELF-ESTEEM

In preparing for your journey, do these five things:

Look at What You've Already Achieved

Think about your life so far, and list the ten best things you've achieved in an "Achievement Log." Perhaps you came top in an important test or exam, played a key role in an important team, produced the best sales figures in a period, did something that made a key difference in someone else's life, or delivered a project that meant a lot for your business. Put these into a smartly formatted document, which you can look at often. And then spend a few minutes each week enjoying the success you've already had.

Think About Your Strengths

Next, use a technique such as SWOT Analysis to take a look at who and where you are. Looking at your Achievement Log, and reflecting on your recent life, think about what your friends would consider to be your strengths and weaknesses. From these, think about the opportunities and threats you may face.

Think about what's Important to You, and Where you Want to Go

Next, think about the things that are really important to you, and what you want to achieve with your life. Setting and achieving goals is a key part of this, and real self-confidence comes from this.

Goal setting is the process you use to set yourself targets, and measure your successful hitting of those targets. Inform your goal setting with your SWOT Analysis.

Set goals that exploit your strengths, minimize your weaknesses, realize your opportunities, and control the threats you face. Having set the major goals in your life, identify the first step in each. Make sure it's a very small step, perhaps taking no more than an hour to complete.

Start Managing Your Mind

At this stage, you need to start managing your mind. Learn to pick up and defeat the negative self-talks which can destroy your confidence.

And Then Commit Yourself to Success!

The final part of preparing for the journey is to make a promise to yourself that you are absolutely committed to your journey, and that you will do all in your power to achieve it.

If, as you're doing it, you find doubts starting to surface write them down and challenge them calmly and rationally. If they dissolve under scrutiny, that's great. However if they are based on genuine risks, make sure you set additional goals to manage these appropriately.

STEP 2: SETTING OUT

This is where you start, ever so slowly, moving towards your goal. By doing the right things, and starting with small, easy wins, you'll put yourself on the path to success – and start building the self-confidence that comes with this.

Build the Knowledge You need to Succeed

Looking at your goals, identify the skills you'll need to achieve them. And then look at how you can acquire these skills confidently and well. Don't just accept a sketchy, just-good-enough solution – look for a solution, a program or a course that fully equips you to achieve what you want to achieve and, ideally, gives you a certificate or qualification you can be proud of.

Focus on the Basics

When you're starting, don't try to do anything clever or elaborate. And don't reach for perfection – just enjoy doing simple things successfully and well.

Set Small Goals, and Achieve Them

Starting with the very small goals you identified in step 1, get in the habit of setting them, achieving them, and celebrating that achievement. Don't make goals particularly challenging at this stage, just get into the habit of achieving them and celebrating them. And, little by little, start piling up the successes!

PILLARS OF SUPERVISOR SELF-ESTEEM

Keep Managing Your Mind

Stay on top of that positive thinking, keep celebrating and enjoying success, and keep those mental images strong.

And on the other side, learn to handle failure. Accept that mistakes happen when you're trying something new. In fact, if you get into the habit of treating mistakes as learning experiences, you can (almost) start to see them in a positive light. After all, there's a lot to be said for the saying "if it doesn't kill you, it makes you stronger."

STEP 3: ACCELERATING TOWARDS SUCCESS

By this stage, you'll feel your self-confidence building. This is the time to start stretching yourself. Make the goals a bit bigger and the challenges a bit tougher. Increase the size of your commitment. And extend the skills you've proven into new, but closely related arenas.

As long as you keep on stretching yourself enough, but not too much, you'll find your self-confidence building apace. What's more, you'll have earned your self-confidence – because you'll have put in the hard graft necessary to be successful.

CHAPTER 2: THOUGHT AWARENESS

Quite often, the way we feel about a situation comes from our perception of it. Often that perception is right, but sometimes it isn't.

For instance, sometimes we're unreasonably harsh with ourselves, or we can jump to wrong conclusion about people's motives. This can cause problems and make us unhappy, and it can lead us to be unfair to others. Thought Awareness, Rational Thinking, and Opportunity Seeking are simple tools that help you turn this around.

A commonly accepted definition of stress, developed by Richard S. Lazarus, is that it occurs when someone thinks that the demands on them "exceed the personal and social resources that the individual is able to mobilize."

In becoming stressed, people must make two main judgments:

1. First, they must feel threatened by the situation.
2. They must judge whether their capabilities and resources are sufficient to meet the threat.

How stressed someone feels depends on how much damage they think the situation can cause them, and how far their resources meet the demands of the situation.

Perception is key to this as (technically) situations are not stressful in their own right. Rather it's our interpretation of the situation that drives the level of stress that we feel.

Quite obviously, sometimes we are right in what we say to ourselves. Some situations may actually be dangerous, and may threaten us physically, socially, or in our career. Here, stress and emotion are part of the "early warning system" that alerts us to the threat from these situations.

Very often, however, we are overly harsh and unjust to ourselves, in a way that we would never be with friends or team members. This, along with other negative thinking, can cause intense stress and unhappiness, and can severely undermine our self-confidence.

What is Thought Awareness?

You're thinking negatively when you fear the future, put yourself down, criticize yourself for errors, doubt your abilities, or expect failure. Negative thinking damages your confidence, harms your performance, and paralyzes your mental skills.

A major problem with this is that negative thoughts tend to flit into our consciousness, do their damage and flit back out again, with their significance having barely been noticed. Since we do not challenge them, they can be completely incorrect and wrong.

However, this does not diminish their harmful effect. Thought Awareness is the process by which you observe your thoughts and become aware of what is going through your head.

One way to become more aware of your thoughts is to observe your stream of consciousness as you think about a stressful situation. Do not suppress any thoughts: instead, just let them run their course while you watch them. Another more general approach to Thought Awareness comes with logging stress in a Stress Diary.

One of the benefits of using a Stress Diary is that, for one or two weeks, you log all of the unpleasant things in your life that cause you stress. This will include negative thoughts and anxieties, and can also include difficult or unpleasant memories and situations that you perceive as negative.

By logging your negative thoughts for a reasonable period of time, you can quickly see patterns in your negative thinking. When you analyze your diary at the end of the period, you should be able to see the most common and most damaging thoughts. Tackle these as a priority. Thought awareness is the first step in the process of managing negative thoughts, as you can only manage thoughts that you're aware of.

Rational Thinking

The next step in dealing with negative thinking is to challenge the negative thoughts that you identified using the Thought Awareness technique. Look at every thought you wrote down and rationally challenge it. Ask yourself whether the thought is reasonable, and does it stand up to fair scrutiny?

As an example, by analyzing your Stress Diary you might identify that you have frequently had the following negative thoughts:
- Feelings of inadequacy.
- Worries that your performance in your job will not be good enough.
- An anxiety that things outside your control will undermine your efforts.
- Worries about other people's reactions to your work.

Starting with these, you might challenge these negative thoughts in the ways shown:

- Feelings of inadequacy: Have you trained and educated yourself as well as you reasonably should to do the job? Do you have the experience and resources you need to do it? Have you planned, prepared and rehearsed appropriately? If you've done all of this, then you've done everything that you should sensible do. If you're still worried, are you setting yourself unattainably high standards for doing the job?

- Worries about performance: Do you have the training that a reasonable person would think is needed to do a good job? Have you planned appropriately? Do you have the information and resources that you need? Have you cleared the time you need, and cued up your support team appropriately? Have you prepared thoroughly? If you haven't, then you need to do these things quickly. If you have, then you are well positioned to give the best performance that you can.

- Problems with issues outside your control: Have you conducted appropriate contingency planning? Have you thought through and managed all likely risks and contingencies appropriately? If so, you will be well prepared to handle potential problems.

• Worry about other people's reactions: If you have put in good preparation, and you do the best you can, then that is all that you need to know. If you perform as well as you reasonably can, and you stay focused on the needs of your audience, then fair people are likely to respond well. If people are not fair, then this is something outside your control.

Opportunity Seeking

Where you have used Rational Thinking to challenge incorrect negative thinking, it's often useful to use rational positive thoughts and affirmations to counter them. It's also useful to look at the situation and see if there are any opportunities that are offered by it.

Affirmations help you to build self-confidence.

By basing your affirmations on the clear, rational assessments of facts that you made using Rational Thinking, you can undo the damage that negative thinking may have done to your self-confidence.

Positive affirmations might be:

• **Feelings of inadequacy**: "I am well trained for this. I have the experience, the tools, and the resources that I need. I have thought-through and prepared for all possible issues. I can do a really good job."

• **Worries about performance**: "I have researched and planned well for this, and I thoroughly understand the problem. I have the time, resources and help that I need. I am well prepared to do an excellent job."

• **Problems with issues outside your control**: "We have thought about everything that might reasonably happen, and have planned how we can handle all likely contingencies. Everyone is ready to help where necessary. We are very well placed to react flexibly and effectively to unusual events."

• **Worry about other people's reaction**: "I am well-prepared and am doing the best I can. Fair people will respect this. I will rise above any unfair criticism in a mature and professional way."

As well as allowing you to structure useful affirmations, part of Positive Thinking is to look at opportunities that the situation might offer to you. In the examples above, successfully overcoming these situations will open up opportunities.

PILLARS OF SUPERVISOR SELF-ESTEEM

You'll gain new skills, you'll be seen as someone who can handle difficult challenges, and you may open up new career opportunities.

Make sure that you take the time to identify these opportunities and focus on them as part of your positive thinking.

CHAPTER 3: AFFIRMATIONS

The problem with negative thoughts is that they can be self-fulfilling. Inside our heads, we talk ourselves into believing that we're not good enough. And, because of this, these thoughts drag down our personal lives, our relationships, and our careers.

Consciously doing the opposite, using positive affirmations will drive positive change both in career and life in general.

Purpose

Affirmations are positive, specific statements that help you to overcome self-sabotaging, negative thoughts. They help you visualize, and believe in, what you're affirming to yourself, helping you to make positive changes to your life and career.

While there's limited research into the effectiveness of using affirmations in a general setting, there is evidence that the use of positive affirmations can successfully treat people with low self-esteem, depression, and other mental health conditions.

For instance, in a study by researchers at Northwestern State University, Natchitoches, people who used positive affirmations for two weeks experienced higher self-esteem than at the beginning of the study.

Also, in a study published in the Journal of American College Health, researchers found that women treated with cognitive behavioral techniques, which included use of positive affirmations, experienced a decrease in depressive symptoms and negative thinking. A study by researchers at the

University of Kentucky, Lexington, had similar results, and came to a similar conclusion.

Of course, it's important to realize that although some people have successfully used affirmations to overcome depression and negative thinking, the technique may not work for everyone. Some people may view affirmations as "wishful thinking," or simply looking at the world with an unrealistic perspective. Quite a lot can depend on your mindset.

So try looking at positive affirmations this way - many of us do repetitive exercises to improve our body's physical health and condition. Affirmations are like exercises for our mind and outlook; these positive mental repetitions can reprogram our thinking patterns so that, over time, we begin to think, and act, in a new way.

Giving Praise

You can use affirmations in any situation where you'd like to see a positive change take place. These might include times when you want to:

- Raise your confidence before presentations or important meetings.
- Control negative feelings such as frustration, anger, or impatience.
- Improve your self-esteem.
- Finish projects you've started.
- Improve your productivity.

Affirmations are often more effective when they're paired with other positive thinking and goal-setting techniques. For instance, affirmations work particularly well alongside visualization - instead of just picturing the change we'd like to see with visualization, we're also saying it aloud using a positive affirmation.

Affirmations are also useful when setting personal goals. Once you've identified the goals you'd like to achieve in the short and long term, you can use positive affirmations to help keep yourself motivated in order to achieve them.

Usage

Remember - affirmations are positive statements that help you challenge and overcome negative thinking and self-sabotaging behaviors. They're usually short, positive statements that target a specific area, behavior, or belief that you're struggling with.

Start by thinking of the areas of your life you'd like to change. For instance, do you wish you had more patience? Or better long lasting relationships with your team or colleagues? Or do you want a more productive workday?

Write down several areas or behaviors you'd like to work on. Then, for each of these, come up with a positive, present-tense statement you can repeat to yourself several times a day.

It's also important that your affirmation is credible, believable, and based on a realistic assessment of fact. For instance, imagine you feel bad about the level of pay you're currently receiving. So you begin to use affirmations to raise your confidence about asking for an increase.

However, it probably wouldn't be wise to affirm to yourself that you're going to double your salary: for most people, and most organizations, doubling what you're earning in one go just isn't feasible. Keep it realistic!

After all, if you can't believe the affirmations you're repeating to yourself, it's highly unlikely that they'll have any impact on your life.

Here are some examples of positive affirmations:

- I have plenty of creativity for this project.
- My work will be recognized in a positive way by my boss and colleagues.
- I can do this!
- My opinion is respected and valued by my team.
- I am successful.
- I am honest in my life, and my work.
- I like completing tasks and projects on time.
- I'm grateful for the job I have.
- I enjoy working with my team.
- I'm bringing a positive attitude to work every day.
- I am excellent at what I do.

CHAPTER 4: TOFFLER'S STABILITY ZONES

How many times have you had "one of those days"? You know, when it seems as if everything in your life changed overnight? There are new initiatives at work, learning new procedures, new colleagues to get to know, or a new office location to become familiar with.

At the end of one of those days, it's a huge relief to get home! You walk in the door, and suddenly the stress disappears. You're surrounded by the people you love, by all the comforts of your familiar things. Home is your safe place, and when you're there, the stress of work is far away.

The challenges that arise from change are common. Every time we turn around, it seems like technology has changed, and many people feel pressured to keep up with this fast pace. Do you carry your IPhone or Blackberry everywhere and take working vacations? Instead of relaxing at night, do you use your laptop to catch up even more?
If this sounds like you, you may feel burned out, overworked and overwhelmed.

The good news is that you can create personal "Stability Zones" to help you manage the change in your life. Familiar places, like home or a coffee shop, can become much-needed escapes to let your mind and body re-energize and renew themselves.

Alvin Toffler first presented the concept of personal Stability Zones in his 1971 book, "Future Shock." Although the theory was never accepted academically, it's still interesting and relevant to what many of us face today.

PILLARS OF SUPERVISOR SELF-ESTEEM

Purpose

Toffler's concept is fairly simple. Stability Zones are places or things that make you feel safe, relaxed, and secure. Think of them as buffers – types of protection or defense – against the outside world. When you're in or with your Stability Zone, you feel safe. It's something safe and familiar, something that doesn't change.

And they're not limited to specific places. They can be things, people, objects, or even ideas:

PEOPLE	IDEAS	PLACES	THINGS	ORGANIZATIONS
Offer relaxing peaceful atmosphere when you're with them	Can be anything from religious faith to politics to deeply held beliefs or values	Very common	Could be favorite possessions	A favorite club
They listen to what you have to say and you can be yourself around them	Ideas or values on environmental protection	Home	Well-loved book or family heirloom	Professional group
They have similar values to yours		Can be on a large scale or small scale	Favorite clothes that make you feel good	Any place you can identify with and feel welcome

As an employer or leader, understand the importance of Stability Zones for your staff, and encourage your team to use them often. These can be most helpful when a company is going through a major transition, such as a takeover. But they can also help you and your staff handles the day-to-day stresses of the work environment.

If you work in an environment where others use your desk or workstation when you're not there, it may be hard to have a Place Stability Zone at the office. In this situation, you may want to carry objects with you that create these zones like photographs or you may want to rely more on less physical types such as people or ideas to help you manage change.

Identification

To determine your personal Stability Zones, start by thinking of two or three options for each type listed above. Then, narrow them down by asking yourself these questions:

• **How stable are they**? For example, if you listed a co-worker as a Person Stability Zone, are you sure that person will always be there for you? If you listed a favorite coffee shop as a Place Stability Zone, are you confident that it will be there for a while? Remember, you want places, people, and things that aren't going to change as fast as the rest of the world. Think in terms of constancy, dependability, and comfort.

• **How many of your Stability Zones can be influenced by you**? To what extent are the zones – these people, places, things, and so on – under your control?

• **Do you spend enough time nurturing these Stability Zones**? You may need to invest time developing and maintaining your Stability Zones, especially with the people in your life. If you don't have the time or desire to invest in these relationships, places, and things, then you might find that, over time, they aren't as comforting and constant as you once thought they might be.

• **Will your Stability Zones remain solid and steady over time**? The only thing you can ever really count on is change. Yes, you want stable things in your life that won't change quickly – but the fact is that, eventually, things are going to change. One day, you may discover that your home just isn't big enough, or one of your deeply held beliefs isn't the guiding force it used to be. Are the Stability Zones you've chosen able to endure over time?

CHAPTER 5: FEAR OF FAILURE

Many of us have probably experienced this at one time or another. The fear of failing can be immobilizing – it can cause us to do nothing, and therefore resist moving forward. But when we allow fear to stop our forward progress in life, we're likely to miss some great opportunities along the way.

Causes

To find the causes of fear of failure, we first need to understand what "failure" actually means.

We all have different definitions of failure, simply because we all have different benchmarks, values, and belief systems. A failure to one person might simply be a great learning experience for someone else.

Many of us are afraid of failing, at least some of the time. But fear of failure (also called "atychiphobia") is when we allow that fear to stop us doing the things that can move us forward to achieve our goals.

Fear of failure can be linked to many causes. For instance, having critical or unsupportive parents is a cause for some people. Because they were routinely undermined or humiliated in childhood, they carry those negative feelings into adulthood.

Experiencing a traumatic event at some point in your life can also be a cause. For example, say that several years ago you gave an important presentation in front of a large group, and you did very poorly. The experience might have been so terrible that you developed a fear of failure about other things. And you carry that fear even now, years later.

PILLARS OF SUPERVISOR SELF-ESTEEM

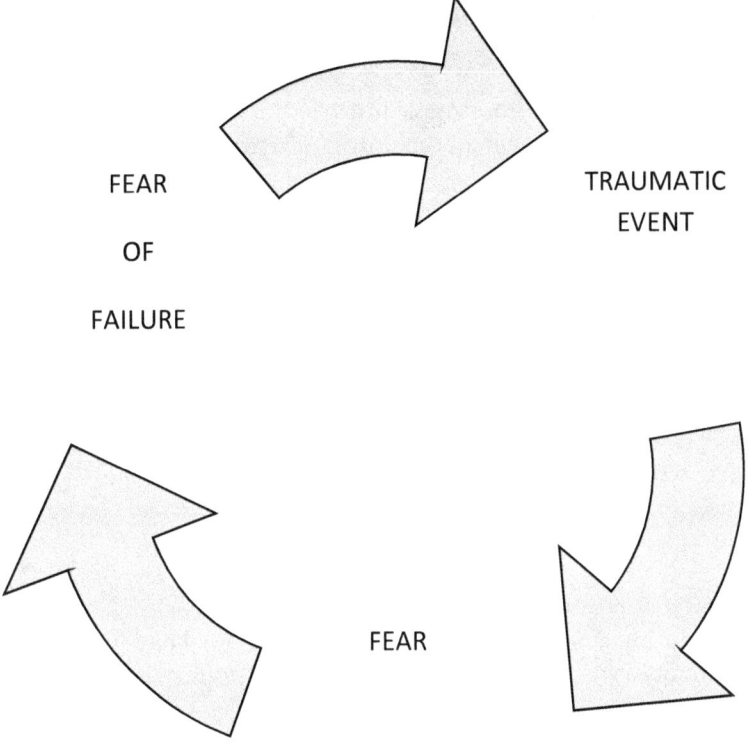

Symptoms

It's almost impossible to go through life without experiencing some kind of failure. People who to do so probably live so cautiously that they go nowhere. Put simply, they're not really living at all.

The wonderful thing about failure is that it's entirely up to us to decide how to look at it. We can choose to see failure as "the end of the world," or as proof of just how inadequate we are. Or, we can look at failure as the incredible learning experience that it often is.

Every time we fail at something, we can choose to look for the lesson we're meant to learn. These lessons are very important; they're how we grow, and how we keep from making that same mistake again. Failures stop us only if we let them.

It's easy to find successful people who have experienced failure. For example:

• Steve Jobs was fired from Apple in 1985. Yet he returned in 1997, and was instrumental in helping the company develop products such as the iMac, iPod, and iPhone.

• Warren Buffet, one of the world's richest and most successful businessmen, was rejected by Harvard University.

• Richard Branson, owner of the Virgin Empire, is a high school dropout.

Most of us will stumble and fall in life. Doors will get slammed in our faces, and we might make some bad decisions. But imagine if Michael Jordan had given up on his dream to play basketball when he was cut from that team.

Imagine if Richard Branson had listened to the people who told him he'd never do anything worthwhile without a high school diploma. Think of the opportunities you'll miss if you let your failures stop you!

Failure can also teach us things about ourselves that we would never have learned otherwise. For instance, failure can help you discover how strong a person you are. Failing at something can help you discover your truest friends, or help you find unexpected motivation to succeed.

Often, valuable insights come only after a failure. Accepting and learning from those insights is key to succeeding in life.

Overcoming

Analyze all potential outcomes – Many people experience fear of failure because they fear the unknown. Remove that fear by considering all of the potential outcomes of your decision.

Learn to think more positively – Positive thinking is an incredibly powerful way to build self-confidence and neutralize self-sabotage

Look at the worse-case scenario – In some cases, the worst case scenario may be genuinely disastrous, and it may be perfectly rational to fear failure. In other cases, however, this worst case may actually not be that bad, and recognizing this can help.

Have a contingency plan – If you're afraid of failing at something, having a "Plan B" in place can help you feel more confident about moving forward.

GOAL SETTING

If you have a fear of failure, you might be uncomfortable setting goals. But goals help us define where we want to go in life. Without goals, we have no sure destination.

Many experts recommend visualization as a powerful tool for goal setting. Imagining how life will be after you've reached your goal is a great motivator to keep you moving forward.

However, visualization might produce the opposite results in people who have a fear of failure. In the article "Tantalizing Fantasies: Positive Imagery Induces Negative Mood in Individuals High in Fear of Failure" (published in the journal Imagination, Cognition and Personality, Vol. 21, No. 4), researcher Thomas Langens showed that people who have a fear of failure were often left in a strong negative mood after being asked to visualize goals and goal attainment.

Start by setting a few small goals. These should be goals that are slightly, but not overwhelmingly, challenging. Think of these goals as "early wins" that are designed to help boost your confidence.

Try to make your goals tiny steps on the route to much bigger goals. Taking one small step at a time will help build your confidence, keep you moving forward, and prevent you from getting overwhelmed with visions of your final goal.

CHAPTER 6: THE PERMA MODEL

About

The PERMA Model was developed by respected positive psychologist, Martin Seligman, and was widely published in his influential 2011 book, "Flourish."

"PERMA" stands for the five essential elements that should be in place for us to experience long lasting well-being. These are:

1. Positive Emotion (P)

For us to experience well-being, we need positive emotion in our lives. Any positive emotion like peace, gratitude, satisfaction, pleasure, inspiration, hope, curiosity, or love falls into this category – and the message is that it's really important to enjoy yourself in the here and now, just as long as the other elements of PERMA are in place.

2. Engagement (E)

When we're truly engaged in a situation, task, or project, we experience a state of flow: time seems to stop, we lose our sense of self, and we concentrate intensely on the present.

This feels really good! The more we experience this type of engagement, the more likely we are to experience well-being.

3. Positive Relationships (R)

As humans, we are "social beings," and good relationships are core to our well-being. Time-and-again, we see that people who have meaningful, positive relationships with others are happier than those who do not. Relationships really do matter!

4. **Meaning (M)**

Meaning comes from serving a cause bigger than ourselves. Whether this is a specific deity or religion, or a cause that helps humanity in some Way, we all need meaning in our lives to have a sense of well-being.

5. **Accomplishment/Achievement (A)**

Many of us strive to better ourselves in some way, whether we're seeking to master a skill, achieve a valuable goal, or win in some competitive event. As such, accomplishment is another important thing that contributes to our ability to flourish.

P - Positive Emotion
E - Engagement
R - Positive Relationships
M - Meaning
A - Accomplishment/Achievement

Usage

Once you're aware of the things that make up well-being (instead of focusing on happiness alone), it's much easier to live a rich, meaningful life.

POSITIVE EMOTIONS

Although we can't be happy all the time, we need to make sure that we often experience positive emotions such as pleasure, happiness, contentment, peace, joy, and inspiration.

If you feel you're not experiencing enough positive emotions in your life, stop and think about why.

First, look at your career. Do you get to use your talents and strengths in your current role?

Also, take a moment to identify people, events, or things that give you pleasure. For example, imagine you love being outdoors, surrounded by nature; but working in an office means you rarely get to experience this source of happiness. Why not bring plants into your office or cubicle?

The aim here is to find ways to bring positive emotions and enjoyment into your daily routine, and to ensure that you don't keep on putting these things off into a future... that never quite arrives.

ENGAGEMENT

Do you feel engaged in your career? Or do you pursue hobbies and activities that help you slip into the state of flow we talked about earlier?

Engagement is most closely identified with the act of creation, but you can also experience deep engagement when participating in sports, spending time with friends, or working on projects that you're fascinated with.

You can increase your engagement at work by first minimizing distractions and improving concentration. These help you slip into a state of flow. Then, as far as you can, focus on projects that provide an interesting challenge for your skills.

Next, look at your interests. Do you make enough time for personal interests such as a favorite hobby or physical activity? Many of us let this important personal time slip away, especially when we're stressed or overloaded with work. Try to devote plenty of time to activities that make you feel happy and engaged.

POSITIVE RELATIONSHIPS

Do you have positive relationships in your life? These can be with anyone: family, friends, neighbors, or colleagues. Do you wish you had more of these relationships?

You probably spend the majority of your waking hours at work, so it's important to start here if you want to build great relationships. Next, look at your personal life. Do you enjoy the company of your family and friends, and do you find that they're positive and supportive?

If not, then it's important to take the time to understand why. Are you devoting enough time to strengthening these relationships? And do you need to make more of an effort to reach out to your friends and family?

Make a commitment to spend significant time with a friend or family member on a regular basis. Relationships take engagement and hard work, and they're often strengthened only when we make an effort to connect with other people. On the other hand, you can't do much to change people: if your relationships aren't positive, how far should you seek to preserve them?

MEANING

Do you feel that your life and work has meaning? That is, do you feel that you're connected in some way to a cause bigger than yourself?

Most of us want to believe that we're working and living for a greater purpose. So finding meaning is important to our overall sense of well-being.

It's just as important to look for meaning in your personal life - certain activities, such as spending time with our family, volunteering, or performing acts of kindness can really improve our sense of meaning in life. If you feel your own life is lacking meaning, do these things - you'll find them hugely satisfying.

ACCOMPLISHMENTS/ACHIEVEMENT

Accomplishment and achievement might be the trickiest elements of PERMA, simply because it's very easy to take them too far.

For instance, in many societies, achievement is highly valued; and, if we're not busy, it can seem that we're not living up to expectations and living a full life. However, if we continually push ourselves past our limits, we run the risk of "running ourselves ragged" in pursuit of the next achievement. If you suspect you're not devoting enough time or energy to accomplishing your dreams, then start now.

First, identify what you truly want to accomplish in life. If you feel that you're devoting too much time towards your achievements (and thereby throwing the rest of your life out of balance), then it might be time to pull back and focus on other elements of the PERMA Model.

CHAPTER 7: PATIENCE

Many of us are impatient at times. Losing control of our patience hurts not only us, but those around us. Impatience raises our stress level and can even cause physical harm to our bodies. Being impatient can also damage relationships.

Practice

Others often see impatient people as arrogant, insensitive, and impulsive. They can be viewed as poor decision makers, because they make quick judgments or interrupt people. Some people will even avoid impatient people, because of their poor people skills and bad tempers.

People with these personality traits are unlikely to be at the top of the list for promotions to leadership positions. Impatience can even affect relationships at home.

The more patient you are with others, the likelier you are to be viewed positively by your peers and your managers, not to mention your family and friends.

Signs of Impatience

How do you know when you're being impatient? **You will probably experience one of more of the following symptoms:**

- Shallow breathing (short breaths).
- Muscle tension.
- Hand clenching/tightening.

- Jiggling/restless feet.
- Irritability/anger.
- Anxiety/nervousness.
- Rushing.
- Snap/quick decisions.

Triggers

If you experience the symptoms of impatience, your next step is to discover the true cause. Many of us have "triggers." These could be people, phrases, or specific situations (like rush-hour traffic) that regularly cause us to enter an impatient frame of mind.

Make a list of things that cause you to become impatient. If you're having trouble identifying your triggers, use these tips:

- Stop and think about the last time you were impatient. What caused it?
- Ask your family, friends, and co-workers about your impatience. Chances are that they know what gets you "wound up".
- Many people become impatient due to physical factors such as hunger, dehydration, or fatigue. Analyze your body the next time you start to feel impatient. A simple remedy might be a snack and a glass of water!
- Keep a journal with you to record when you start to feel impatient. Write down what the situation is, and why you're getting frustrated.

Identifying your triggers helps because it forces you to examine your actions and uncover why you're doing what you're doing. This knowledge also helps you devise strategies to avoid becoming impatient.

Of course, it would be great if you could avoid the triggers that make you impatient. But for most of us, that's just not possible. So you have to learn to manage impatience instead.

Management

When you feel impatient, it's important to get out of this frame of mind as quickly as possible. Try these strategies:

☐ **Take deep, slow breaths, and count to 10.** Doing this helps slow your heart rate, relaxes your body, and distances you emotionally from the situation. If you're feeling really impatient, you might need to do a longer count, or do this several times.

- **Impatience can cause you to tense your muscles involuntarily.** So, consciously focus on relaxing your body. Again, take slow, deep breaths. Relax your muscles, from your toes up to the top of your head.

- **Learn to manage your emotions.** Remember, you have a choice in how you react in every situation. You can choose to be patient, or choose not to be: it's all up to you.

- **Force yourself to slow down.** Speak and move more slowly. It will appear to others as if you're calm – and, by "acting" patient, you can often "feel" more patient.

- **Practice active listening and empathic listening.** Make sure you give other people your full attention, and patiently plan your response to what they say.

- **Remind yourself that your impatience rarely gets others to move faster** – in fact, it can interfere with other people's ability to perform complex or highly-skilled work. All you're doing is creating more stress, which is completely unproductive.

- **Try to talk yourself out of your impatient frame of mind.** Remind yourself how silly it is that you're reacting this way. People often don't mind if a meeting is delayed, just as long as you let them know that you're running late in advance.

- If your impatience causes you to react in anger toward others, **use anger management techniques to calm down.**

- **Some people become impatient because they're perfectionists.** However, in addition to causing impatience, perfectionism can actually slow productivity and increase stress.

CHAPTER 8: THE ABC TECHNIQUE

About

This approach was originally created by psychologist, Dr. Albert Ellis. It was then adapted by Dr. Martin Seligman, a University of Pennsylvania professor and past president of the American Psychological Association. Seligman's adapted version was published in his 1990 book, "Learned Optimism."

ABC stands for:
- Adversity.
- Beliefs.
- Consequences.

In short, we encounter Adversity (or, an Activating Event, as per Ellis's original model). How we think about this creates Beliefs. These beliefs then influence what we do next, so they become Consequences.

Here's an example - you yell at your assistant because she forgot to print a key report before your meeting (Adversity). You then think, "I'm a really lousy boss" (Belief). You then perform poorly during your meeting, because your self-confidence has plummeted (Consequences).

The key point occurs between adversity and belief. When you encounter adversity, how you tend to explain it to yourself directly impacts your mindset and your relationships. Seligman calls this your "explanatory style," and he says that it is a habit that influences your entire outlook on life.

Resetting the Pattern

STEP 1: TRACK YOUR INNER DIALOG

Begin by keeping a diary for several days. Your goal is to listen to your inner dialog, especially when you encounter a stressful or difficult situation.

For each situation, write down the adversity you experienced, the beliefs you formed after encountering the adversity, and the consequences of those beliefs.

Consequences can be anything, from happy or unhappy thoughts and feelings, to specific actions that you took.

STEP 2: ANALYZE RESULTS

Once you've written down several ABC situations, take a look at what you have found.

Here, you need to look for patterns in your thinking, specifically, how any broad beliefs have led to specific consequences.

To be optimistic, you need to change your beliefs following adversity. This, in turn, leads to more positive consequences

Managing Negative ABC Patterns

As you can see, the beliefs you develop after encountering adversity play a major role in your life, and determine whether you're an optimistic or pessimistic thinker. This makes it important to manage negative ABC patterns.

There are two ways to override these: distraction and disputation.

DISTRACTION

If you want to interrupt your negative thoughts, you need to distract yourself. Simply telling yourself "not to think negatively" isn't going to work: you need to interrupt the cycle.

To do this, try distracting yourself when you start creating negative beliefs.

For example, you could wear a rubber band around your wrist. After you've gone through a stressful situation, and when you begin to formulate negative thoughts and beliefs as a result, snap the rubber band against your skin. This physical sting will remind you to step out of the cycle of negative thinking.

Once you've interrupted your negative thoughts, you need to shift your attention somewhere else. Concentrate intently on something else for a minute.

DISPUTATION

Although distraction is useful for interrupting negative thinking, a more permanent solution is to dispute them. Think of Disputation as a "D" after ABC.

To dispute your negative thoughts and beliefs, you argue with yourself rationally. In particular, you look for the mistaken assumptions about your explanatory style that we talked about earlier.

There are 3 dimensions to your explanatory style:

1. Permanence
Pessimistic people unconsciously assume that the causes of bad events are permanent, while optimists believe that bad events are temporary.

For instance, imagine you had a bad day and had no time to help a colleague who needed your expertise. A pessimist might think, "I should never be friends with anyone at work because I'm a terrible friend." An optimist might think, "I was a terrible friend today."

The difference is subtle, but it really matters for your outlook!

PILLARS OF SUPERVISOR SELF-ESTEEM

2. Pervasiveness

Pessimists make universal statements about their lives when something goes badly, while optimists make specific statements.

For instance, a pessimist might think, "All my reports are useless." An optimist might think, "This report was useless."

Again, the difference is subtle. Pessimists take one negative event and allow it to turn their entire work, or life, into a catastrophe. Optimists recognize that they might have failed in one area, but they don't allow that failure to overwhelm other parts of their lives.

3. Personalization

When we experience a negative event, we have two ways to think about it. We can blame ourselves for the event (internalizing it). Or, we can blame something outside ourselves (externalizing it).

Pessimists often internalize blame. They think, "This is all my fault," or "I'm too dumb to do this job." Optimists have higher self-esteem because they tend to externalize blame, thinking, "This is all John's fault," or "I haven't learnt enough about this skill yet; that's why I'm not doing well at this task."

CHAPTER 9: BURNOUT

What is Burnout?

Two important definitions of burnout are:

• "A state of physical, emotional, and mental exhaustion caused by long term involvement in emotionally demanding situations." – Ayala Pines and Elliot Aronson.

• "A state of fatigue or frustration brought about by devotion to a cause, way of life, or relationship that failed to produce the expected reward." – Herbert J. Freudenberger.

Between them, these definitions embrace the essence of burnout, with the first stressing the part that exhaustion plays in it, and the second focusing on the sense of disillusionment that is at its core.

Anyone can become exhausted. What is so poignant about burnout is that it mainly strikes people who are highly committed to their work: You can only "burn out" if you have been "alight" in the first place.

While exhaustion can be overcome with rest, a core part of burnout is a deep sense of disillusionment, and it is not experienced by people who can take a more cynical view of their work.

Symptoms

- Having a negative and critical attitude at work.
- Dreading going into work, and wanting to leave once you're there.
- Having low energy and little interest at work.
- Having trouble sleeping.
- Being absent from work a lot.
- Having feelings of emptiness.
- Experiencing physical complaints such as headaches, illness, or backache.
- Being irritated easily by team members or clients.
- Having thoughts that your work doesn't have meaning or make a difference.
- Pulling away emotionally from your colleagues or clients.
- Feeling that your work and contribution goes unrecognized.
- Blaming others for your mistakes.
- Thinking of quitting work, or changing roles

Stress & Burnout

So, what's the difference between stress and burnout?

Although the two share some characteristics, there are distinct differences. Stress is often relatively short-term, and it is often caused by a feeling that work is out of control. You might experience stress several days in a row, especially when you're working on a large project or under a tight deadline.

However, once the situation changes, stress often lessens or disappears entirely. (Stress can affect you over the longer-term, however, if you're consistently experiencing these things.)

Burnout often takes place over a longer period. You might experience it if you believe your work is meaningless; when there's a disconnect between what you're currently doing and what you truly want to be doing; or when things change for the worse – for example, when you lose a supportive boss, or when your workload increases beyond a sustainable point. You go through "the motions" instead of being truly engaged. Over time, this leads to cynicism, exhaustion, and, sometimes, poor performance.

People experience burnout for a variety of reasons. Lack of autonomy is a common cause, so you might experience burnout if you don't have much control over your work, or if you feel that you never have enough time to finish tasks and projects.

Another common cause is when your values don't align with the actions, behaviors, or values of your organization, or of your role.

Other causes include:

- Having unclear goals or job expectations.
- Working in a dysfunctional team or organization.
- Experiencing an excessive workload.
- Having little or no support from your boss or organization.
- Lacking recognition for your work.
- Having monotonous or low-stimulation work.

Clearly, the consequences of burnout can be severe. Your productivity can drop dramatically; and this not only impacts your career, but it negatively impacts your team and organization as well.

Your creativity will also be affected, so you're less likely to spot opportunities (and you don't have the interest or desire to act on them), and you may find excuses to miss work or take days off sick.

Career burnout can also spill over into your personal life, negatively impacting your well-being and your relationships with friends and family.

Avoiding Burnout

When burnout starts to occur, many people focus on short-term solutions to compensate for the feelings. While this can certainly help, the relief is often only temporary. You also need to focus on strategies that will have a deeper impact, and create lasting change.

1. Work with Purpose

Do you feel that your career has a deeper purpose, other than just earning a paycheck? Most of the time, rediscovering your purpose can go a long way towards helping you avoid burnout and keeping stress at bay.

Look at the deeper impact of what you do every day; how does your work make life better for other people? How could you add more meaning to what you do every day?

These are important questions, so spend time thinking deeply on them.

If you think that you're in the wrong role or career, develop a career strategy to help you plan for a career that's better for you. Or, use job crafting to shape your role, so that it fits you better.

2. Perform a Job Analysis

When you experience work overload day in and day out, you can start to feel as if you're on a treadmill and that you'll never catch up. This is demoralizing, stressful, and often leads to burnout.

Perform a job analysis so you can clarify what's expected of you, and what isn't. This tool will help you identify what's truly important in your role, so that you can cut out or delegate tasks that aren't as essential.

If you feel that your boss is assigning more work than you can handle, then schedule a private meeting to discuss the issue. Let him or her know that your excessive workload is leading to burnout. Come prepared with some options that could be considered for shifting certain tasks or projects to someone else.

You can also make life easier by learning how to manage conflicting priorities and deal with unreasonable demands.

3. "Give" to Others

One quick and easy way to add meaning to your career is to give to others, or to help them in small ways. When you do this, it makes you feel good. Even the smallest act of kindness can re-energize you and help you find meaning in your work.

4. Take Control

You can avoid or overcome burnout by finding ways to create more autonomy in your role. Try talking with your boss to see if he or she is willing to let you have more control over your tasks, projects, or deadlines.

You'll also feel more in control of your work if you manage your time effectively. Learn prioritization techniques, and make use of To-Do Lists or an Action Program to take control of your day. Then tie these in with daily, weekly, monthly, and yearly personal goals.

5. Exercise Regularly

Exercise can help alleviate stress and create a sense of well-being. You will also experience increased energy and productivity when you exercise regularly. What's more, regular exercise will help you get a good night's sleep.

Get more exercise by getting up earlier, or even by exercising at lunchtime. You might also be more motivated to exercise by teaming up with colleagues, or by setting up an office fitness challenge.

6. Learn to Manage Stress

When not managed well, short-term stress can contribute to burnout. This is why you should learn how to manage stress effectively.

There are several strategies that you can use to cope with stress. For instance, you could keep a stress diary to document what routinely causes you stress. Practicing deep breathing, meditation, and other relaxation techniques can help you calm down when you're experiencing stress.

You can also manage the way you think – this can contribute to stress. By monitoring your thoughts and practicing positive thinking, you can change unhelpful reactions and manage your emotions through a stressful situation.

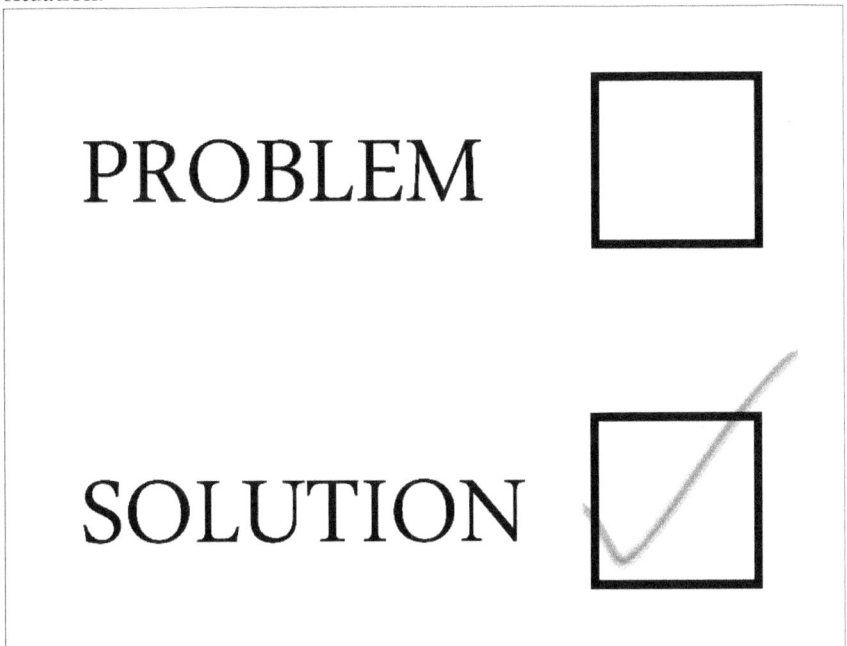

CHAPTER 10: STRESS MANAGEMENT

No matter what you do or where you work, it's likely that you'll have experienced environmental distractions during the day. If unaddressed, these can contribute to the levels of stress you experience.

Work space stress can come from any physical conditions that you perceive as irritating, frustrating, uncomfortable, or unpleasant.

Sources of work space stress include the following:

- Poor lighting.
- Loud background noise, such as music, traffic noise, or conversation.
- Chairs or desks that cause discomfort, or even repetitive strain injuries (RSI).
- Unhealthy air, such as air pollution, smoke, or unpleasant smells.
- Overcrowding or workstations in close proximity to others.
- Long, difficult, or crowded commutes.
- Uncomfortable climate conditions, such as an office that is too hot, too cold, too humid, or too dry.
- An unclean or cluttered office space.

Some of these are quite small things, but, taken together, they can significantly contribute to the stress that people experience.

Workplace Stress Management

There are several things that you can do to lessen or eliminate sources of stress in your workplace. While you can make some of these changes on your own, you might need your boss's permission for others.

REDUCE OFFICE NOISE

Noise is a harmful source of stress. People often cite background noise, or a lack of sound privacy, as the most distracting element in work environments. One study found that office noise, particularly telephones ringing at empty desks and loud conversations, impaired worker concentration. Another study found that workers experienced a drop in motivation and in their ability to solve problems when exposed to low-intensity office noise.

You can reduce noise pollution in your work area in several ways.

First, consider closing your office door when you need to focus. A closed door helps you to minimize distractions, both audible and visual. However, if your organization has an "open door" policy, or if you work in a cubicle, this won't be an option.

Consider using headphones while you're working. Listening to music, especially classical or ambient music will eliminate distractions and can improve your concentration. Alternatively, you can play audio tracks of waterfalls, birds chirping, or white noise to reduce the distraction of background noise.

If you work in an open office, ask your boss about installing noise screens. These block and absorb background noise and create a quiet space. You can also use carpets, rugs, or fabric on surfaces and walls to absorb sound.

Plants are an important addition to any office. Not only do they reduce air pollution and add oxygen to the atmosphere, but they also reduce background noise. Some plants, such as peace lilies or weeping figs, are more effective for dampening noise than others.

Place plants around the edges or corners of a space for the best sound dampening effect. You'll notice a bigger difference if you use several smaller arrangements in a space, rather than one big cluster of plants.

If your colleagues regularly play music or talk loudly on the phone, ask them politely and assertively to be quieter. Keep in mind that any noise you make in your office might be a source of environmental stress for someone else, so do your best to work quietly.

CREATE A HEALTHY WORKSTATION

You may spend much of your day sitting at your desk in front of a computer. This is why it's so important that your chair, desk, and computer are at the correct height and angle.

When these tools are routinely out of alignment, you might suffer from repetitive strain injury. This potentially serious condition occurs when you engage in prolonged, repetitive movements such as typing, clicking a mouse, or writing. RSI can result in damage to muscles, tendons, and nerves in the neck, shoulders, wrists, or hands.

Good posture at your desk is an important part of reducing or eliminating RSI.

Ideally, you should follow these guidelines when at your desk:

- Sit with your feet flat on the floor, with your knees directly over your feet. Your knees should be bent at a right angle, or slightly greater, and they should overhang the chair's end by two or three inches.
- Your lower back should be arched in, perhaps supported by your chair. Your upper back should be naturally rounded.
- When typing, your elbows should be bent at, or slightly greater than, 90 degrees. Your mouse should be located very close to your computer, so that you don't have to lean or stretch to reach it.
- Your computer screen should be directly in front of you, not off to the side. It should be no more than 15 to 25 inches from your eyes.
- Take frequent breaks to move around when you're working. Prolonged sitting in a fixed position can affect your health and contribute to RSI. Walk around for at least five minutes in every hour.

Proper lighting is also an important element of a healthy workplace. If the light in your office is too dim, you risk straining your eyes. Poor lighting can also contribute to back pain, since you might unconsciously and repeatedly lean forward to see more clearly.

Make sure that your office is well-lit with lamps, or, ideally, with plenty of natural light. Move your desk closer to a window, and open the blinds to let in as much light as possible. If bushes or trees are blocking the light, consider having them trimmed.

However, keep in mind that direct light in your eyes, or on your computer screen, will cause you to squint and can make working difficult.

CLEAN AND ORGANIZE YOUR OFFICE

A cluttered, disorganized office can be a considerable source of stress, especially when you can't find what you need, or when the office isn't cleaned thoroughly because of clutter.

Take time to get organized. You might want do this before the workday starts, when colleagues or urgent tasks are less likely to distract you. Although no one likes an earlier than usual start, you'll be more productive as a result.

Honestly assess what you need in your office and what you don't. Recycle papers and files that don't contribute to your work, and prioritize those that do. Go through your filing system and make sure that it's organized and that you can quickly find what you need.

Your office or work space should be a pleasant space. Do whatever you can to make it comfortable and enjoyable. This might mean getting your boss's permission to paint the walls a bright color, putting up soothing or meaningful artwork, or adding a small desktop fountain. The more pleasant and comfortable your work space is the more enjoyable and productive your workday will be.

LOOK AT YOUR COMMUTE

Whether you drive or use public transportation, your commute can add stress to your day. It can also have a negative effect on your working relationships and productivity.

One study found that stressful commutes caused participants to express more hostility and aggression at work. Another found that professionals with a long commute were more likely to experience back pain, fatigue, and worry, compared with those who had shorter commutes.

Lessen the stress of your commute by preparing for it the night before. Lay out the clothes that you want to wear, and prepare your lunch. Try to leave early, so that you can beat the rush.

Use your commuting time to relax or learn something new. Listen to music, audio books, or podcasts, or read a book (if you take public transportation). Take different routes to work; while some routes might be longer, you might arrive at the same time if there is less traffic. The variety and reduced stress might be worth the extra distance.

Think about setting up a carpool at work, or in your neighborhood. Commuting with others means that you can rest on the days when someone else is driving, and sharing the ride lessens costs and stress for everyone involved.

Exercise is also important for handling a stressful commute. You can exercise into your busy schedule by walking during your lunch break, or even by joining a gym near to your office. By going to the gym straight after work, you'll avoid the rush hour and arrive home feeling peaceful and energized.

Ask your boss whether you can telecommute one or two days a week, in order to reduce the effects of your commute. Or, see if you can set up a flex-time arrangement that allows you to work slightly different hours; even coming in an hour earlier and leaving an hour earlier can spare you much of the stress of a rush-hour commute.

Last, if your commute is long and particularly unpleasant, consider moving closer to your office.

ABOUT THE AUTHORS

ANGELA L. ANFIELD:
Facilitator/Instructional
Designer

I really enjoy working with others in developing their full potential. There is no greater reward than having those you've taken under your wing, develop and flourish.

Angela is the Director of Operations, of Pillars of Training, Inc. She holds a degree in Law Enforcement and Protection, as well as almost twenty years of experience and training in self-esteem.

DAVID J. SAMSON
Facilitator/Instructional
Designer

As an educator, my favorite thing to see is that 'ah-ha' moment in students. There is no way to know everything, but we have a chance to know the right things for us.

David is the CEO of Pillars of Training, Inc. He holds a Bachelor of Adult Education from Brock University, as well as over 23 years of instruction experience and 15 in a supervisory role

www.ingramcontent.com/pod-product-compliance
Lightning Source LLC
Chambersburg PA
CBHW071826170526
45167CB00003B/1434